RAILWAYS OF SCOTLAND
IN THE LATTER DAYS OF STEAM

Malcolm Castledine

BOOK LAW PUBLICATIONS

The Author with 60010 at Ferryhill engine shed, 20th July 1964.

First published in the United Kingdom
by Book Law Publications 2004
382 Carlton Hill, Nottingham, NG4 1JA
Printed and bound by The Amadeus Press, Cleckheaton, West Yorkshire.

INTRODUCTION

During the latter days of steam on British Railways I managed to visit Scotland three times, twice on holidays with my parents in 1963 and 1964, and under my own steam, with the help of a Freedom of Scotland ticket, in 1966. Each time I was equipped with at least one camera and hopefully managed to capture, on film, the railway scene north of the Border during those transition years. Each trip was taken during the month of July so lighting conditions were usually fairly good and the long daylight hours allowed me to get more into the day than usual.

The 1963 and 1964 visits were done by car and although my parents were good enough to take me to some of the less photogenic locations in Scotland (speaking as a tourist perhaps) I still had to 'holiday' with them for much of the time. The first 'expedition' started via the Lake District where, on the 7th July 1963 we stopped off at Ravenglass and took in the miniature railway there with of course a trip on the little trains to get us in the mood. Two days later we were in Fort William where I managed to have a look around the engine shed and expose a few frames of film, copping one of the rare Fowler 4F's, 44255 which had been the snowplough engine and last steam locomotive in the Highlands. It was withdrawn and stored, awaiting movement to a scrap merchant, so I didn't catch it in steam.

For the next four days we followed the tourist trail and my camera was

Ex-LMS 4F No.44255 at Fort William, 9th July 1963. Note the tender - essential equipment for snow plough duties.

redundant. However, the family car enabled us to cover some vast distances (by 1963 standards) which would have been impossible using public transport alone. On the 14th we arrived in Perth whereupon a visit to the engine shed enabled me to bag some of the older ex Caley engines still extant. Later in the day we motored north and west to Loch Tay where at the western end of that loch we got to Killin a small village nestling amongst some of the higher peaks of the UK. We based ourselves in Killin for another couple of days and this enabled me to visit the still operative branch line which had an engine shed to boot although the one resident engine did become a bit boring after ten portraits; those pictures are now looked upon with a more sympathetic eye some forty years on.

From Loch Tay we drove south to Stirling on the

17th where my photographic permit allowed a visit around the shed and a good look at its occupants. Then east to Bo'ness to have a look at the infamous 'dump' I had heard and read so much about. At that time it was difficult to comprehend so many 'dead' engines in one place, however, it was the shape of things to come. A trip to Scotland would not be complete without a look at the Forth railway bridge - what a sight. I even managed to photograph a goods train negotiating its seemingly myriad maze of metalwork.

We got to Edinburgh in time for me to visit all three of the main engine sheds. Now the holiday was really starting for me but, alas, it was actually drawing to a close. No matter, I went to Haymarket first, then on to Dalry Road where some old timers were laid up. Next was St Margarets via Waverley station. The former North British shed was, as expected, a busy place with many of the East Coast's former star engines cold, silent and no longer required no that the main line diesels had taken their work on the express passenger trains. but it wasn't all doom and gloom at St Margarets. these depot was still vibrant and would be for a couple of years longer.

The 18th of July was to be my last chance in 1963 to savour the steam railway in Scotland so I spent the day at Edinburgh Waverley station and alongside the main line where it passes Princes Street Gardens. A4's, A3's, A2's and A1's all appeared for my camera with V2's of course and a host of other steam classes in amongst the diesels.

The 1964 holiday was another July event, and the first shed visited was Dumfries on the 12th but during our journey through Northern

England on the 11th we stopped off at Hellifield, Windermere and Oxenholme. After Dumfries we had eight days of railway-free holiday, all the time motoring north. On the 20th my 'holiday' really started, at Aberdeen of all places. Ferryhill shed in July 1964 was the centre of the A4 universe and I admit that all of my film that day, except for two frames, was used up on Gresley's streamlined Pacifics - no less than eight of them were on shed, seemingly for my enjoyment only. Next day we got to Perth where another visit to the shed found a mainly, as expected, LMS allocation resident. There seemed to be more BR Standard's than before but perhaps that was my imagination. We stayed overnight in Perth and after an early start visited Dundee Tay Bridge shed and then went south to Stirling to overnight there. Besides, a couple of North British 0-6-0s, Tay Bridge had some Peppercorn A2's to offer amongst the B1's, V2's and BR Standard's. Stirling did not have much to offer other than ex LMS engines.

On the 23rd Bathgate shed was visited first with J36 and J37 0-6-0s being to the fore. On to Edinburgh and Dalry Road was next, Haymarket was, at the time, undergoing rebuilding to a diesel depot and steam was non-existent there so it had no interest for me. The old timers from last year's visit had gone but what a surprise to see 60007 on shed in steam amongst the Stanier Cl.5's. Finally, St Margarets where exLNER Pacifics were a bit thin on the ground but still in residence. Again former LMS engines were to be seen. The visit to Edinburgh brought to an end my 1964 holiday. The following year the locomotives of southern England got my attention, however, that is another story.

In 1966 I was still serving my time as an engineering apprentice (steam plant of course) and to keep tradition going I booked my annual holidays for the July period. This particular year I decided to first visit the Southern Region for a week then return to Scotland for a week, on my own, to have a look at the changes which had taken place over the previous two years of my absence, and particularly to see the last of Gresley's A4's on the Aberdeen-Glasgow 3-hour expresses. Not then having my own motor vehicle it was only natural for me to travel by train and so I

purchased a Southern Region Rail Rover and a Freedom of Scotland ticket from British Railways and set off on my fourteen day expedition armed with lots of film and two cameras. I remember being in Southampton on the 15th July and Glasgow on the 17th so on the 16th I made a twelve hour journey by train from Bournemouth to Edinburgh (Waverley), via Waterloo, Euston and Glasgow (Central).

Eastfield shed was the first to be visited and here the transition was in progress to a diesel depot with little active steam around the place, what few engines were on site were mainly 'dead' on their way to works or scrapyards. Corkerhill was next and it was pretty much the same at this shed. Polmadie had a lot of engines stored but it did offer quite a number of live ones, a lot of which were visiting.

The morning of the 18th found me in Alloa to try and catch on film the Kincardine power station coal trains which at that time had mainly WD and J38 haulage. A good morning session with the camera saw me happy enough and later that afternoon I was visiting Stirling to see the 1.30 p.m. Aberdeen to Glasgow 3-hour express make its call. In the meantime I was invited into Alloa signal box where over a few cups of coffee I chatted with the 'bobby'. One of the good things about being on my own was being able to indulge in railway talk with interested railway staff without having to watch time. However, during my stint in the box, word came through that the diesel multiple unit due to take me from Alloa to Stirling had been derailed which had put a spanner in the works, or so I thought. The Station Master at Alloa decided to charter a double decker bus from Alexander's to take his passengers on to Stirling. The 'passengers' on the double-decker were myself and one other person, a young lady. Everything was going fine until just after we passed Cambus when the young lady signalled to the driver that she did not want to go to Stirling and had booked for one of the intermediate stations (Cambus) at which point the driver turned the bus around and headed back down the road for a mile or so before turning down a narrow country lane (short cut to Cambus), all the time seemingly exceeding the speed limit in this dilapidated old banger. However, he got the lady to her destination and then we retraced

our steps even faster, getting me to Stirling in time to catch Peppercorn A2 No.60532 arriving at Stirling with the 1.30 p.m. from Aberdeen.

Travelling on to Aberdeen I spent most of the 19th at both the station and the shed where the A4 count was now down to just two engines: 60019 and 60034. No.60532 was also back on shed after its trip to Glasgow.

On Wednesday 20th I went to Dundee where things had not changed too much over the last two years. Perth shed also yielded much the same types as before but there was less of them, most were in store, the diesels having muscled in well and truly. On Thursday I reached Thornton Junction shed in the morning and spent a number of hours there taking in the sights. Later in the afternoon I got to Dunfermline shed where once again Scottish hospitality shone through and the Foreman had J36 No.65288 pulled out from the back of the shed on to the yard for me to photograph in the evening sun.

My final day in Scotland was spent, as was tradition by now it seems, at St Margarets shed where there was still hustle and bustle but no Pacifics - V2's keeping the Gresley flag flying but not for much longer. Later that day a quick visit to Motherwell shed was crammed in before I headed south for home happy on the one hand, that I had managed to see and do so much on a somewhat whirlwind tour, but sad on the other hand knowing that the next time I was to visit Scotland there would be no steam sheds nor any steam. Luckily, I have a lot of the moments of those Scottish trips on film and herein I hope you too will enjoy those moments as much as I did all that time ago.

Malcolm Castledine, Long Eaton 2004.

Ferryhill based Stanier Class 5 No.44703 (substituting for 60532 which was having a boiler wash) departs from Aberdeen with the 1.30 p.m. express for Glasgow (Buchanan Street) on a glorious Tuesday 19th July 1966. The rake for these trains consisted the then BR Standard Mk.1 coaching stock with a restaurant car some four vehicles behind the engine. Allocated to Aberdeen since July 1955, this engine was a regular performer on these expresses. New in September 1948, No.44703 went first to St Rollox shed then, in May 1951, it moved to Carlisle Kingmoor before moving north to Ferryhill. Five months after this scene was captured the engine moved to Perth shed from where it was condemned in December. By May 1967 it was in the hands of scrap merchant J.McWilliam William at Shettleston.

60034 LORD FARINGDON at the head of one of the 3-hour expresses which plied between Aberdeen and Glasgow over mainly former Caledonian lines. This A4 was only five weeks away from withdrawal when photographed on Tuesday 19th July 1966 standing in Aberdeen station awaiting departure to Glasgow with the 5.15 p.m. train. Although condemned at Ferryhill shed, 60034 took the long journey south for scrapping at Blyth during the following October.

(right) A more dramatic, though stationary view of 60034 at Ferryhill.

During the period when the Gresley A4's were drafted to Aberdeen to work the accelerated three-hour Aberdeen-Glasgow expresses, no less than fourteen of the class were allocated to Ferryhill shed at one time or another, whilst two more (No.60031 from 3rd February 1962 to its 29th October 1965 condemnation, and 60027 from 20th May 1962 to 6th September 1964) found a home in Glasgow at St Rollox (Balornock) shed to help balance those workings. These sixteen engines, along with the rest of the class, had been the mainstay of the main line express passenger train workings on the East Coast route until the appearance of the English Electric 'Deltic' diesel-electric locomotives which ousted them from those duties and although withdrawals of the A4's was imminent, it was realised that many of the class were still capable of a few years hard work hence their move. The fact that many of them worked into 1966 no doubt had a bearing on the fact that four of them later went on to be preserved; something that perhaps might not have happened had they been withdrawn a few years previously. The Ferryhill engines did not all arrive at that shed together and instead they trickled in between 1962 and 1965, and not all of them were in peak condition with some serving just a few months before being withdrawn for scrap. Of course these were not the first LNER Pacifics allocated to Ferryhill, prior to this mini migration there were, from early BR days and onwards, the Thompson and Peppercorn versions of the A2 based for long periods. The table below shows the arrival, departure and eventual disposal dates of the fourteen Ferryhill A4 engines.

No.	Arrival 61B.	Departure	Disposal.
60004	11th June 1962	20th September 1962	*To Haymarket.*
	17th June 1963	17th July 1966 *condemned.*	Scrap (a).
60005	10th November 1963	12th March 1964 *condemned.*	Scrap (d).
60006	4th May 1964	3rd September 1965 *condemned.*	Scrap (a).
60007	20th July 1964	1st February 1966.	Preserved.
60009	20th May 1962	1st June 1966.	Preserved.
60010	20th October 1963	29th May 1965.	Preserved.
60011	11th June 1962	11th May 1964 *condemned.*	Scrap (c).
60012	20th January 1964	20th August 1964 *condemned.*	Scrap (a).
60016	10th November 1963	19th March 1965 *condemned.*	Scrap (a).
60019	10th November 1963	5th September 1966.	Preserved.
60023	17th May 1964	30th October 1964 *condemned.*	Scrap (a).
60024	6th May 1965	5th September 1966 *condemned.*	Scrap (b).
60026	13th April 1964	21st December 1965 *condemned.*	Scrap (b).
60034	17th May 1964	24th August 1966 *condemned.*	Scrap (b).

Scrapping venues:
(a)   **Motherwell Machinery & Scrap, Wishaw.**
(b)   **Hughes, Bolckow, Blyth.**
(c)   **Darlington works.**
(d)   **G.H.Campbell, Airdrie.**

LORD FARINGDON on shed at Ferryhill in July 1966 coaled and ready to back down to the station for a another southbound working. Throughout its two year stint at Aberdeen, this engine had a non-corridor tender (No.5640) attached but when it went for scrap a corridor type tender (No.5329) was attached.

LORD FARINGDON nameplate. Just look at the state of the casing and paintwork.

On an earlier visit to Aberdeen, No.60023 GOLDEN EAGLE was captured on Ferryhill shed yard on Monday 20th July 1964 in a similar pose to 60034. Note the BRCW Type 2 diesel locomotive poking out of the shed; both these and the BR built Type 2's were regular visitors to Aberdeen from Inverness during this period though none were allocated to Ferryhill at the time.

60034 again (right) but at an earlier date, 20th July 1964, in the company of 60010 DOMINION OF CANADA. Both engines are going through servicing though cleaning was not to be part of that routine, whilst the shed foreman observes the proceedings. The diesel shunter in the background is yet another visitor though this time from nearby Kittybrewster shed which had fifteen of them allocated in this period. During my travels I rarely took any photographs of individual diesels preferring instead to snap as many steam locomotives as possible and those diesels which do show up are usually in the background. With hindsight I should have made the effort to capture these transition period diesels on film but existing on an apprentice's wage, film was always at a premium so I chose steam every time knowing that the latter had only a few more years before they all disappeared whereas the former would be around long afterwards! Anyway, diesels did not excite or interest me then or even now for that matter.

A classic front three-quarter view of Stanier Class 5 No.44704 being coaled-up at the Ferryhill stage in July 1964. This was a Perth engine and except for its first month in service from new at Carstairs shed, it was to spend all its working life at 63A. Looking to be in need of a good clean, this locomotive was to have another two years and two months service in front of it at the time this scene was captured.

Virtually two years later, and in the same position, Ferryhill resident Class 5 No.44794 is also caught being coaled at what by now appears to be a refurbished coaling stage. Considering that steam was nearly finished at Ferryhill the reasons for recladding the front screen wall with new corrugated iron sheets must have been serious to warrant such expenditure. This rear three-quarter view shows off the riveted tender nicely with lots of detail discerned. This engine had started its working life at Polmadie shed in August 1947 and had moved to Aberdeen in September 1954. Two months after this photograph the 'Black 5' moved to Perth where in April of the following year it was withdrawn. By September 1967 it was in the hands of Motherwell Machinery & Scrap who by them were quite expert at reducing one hundred plus tons of metal to tiny pieces ready for the blast furnace.

The A4's were not the easiest of locomotives to maintain but the Ferryhill fitters did a superb job keeping their small fleet of 'Streaks' in good condition. On 19th July 1966 BITTERN is undergoing remedial work which was possibly the last before it was withdrawn and purchased for preservation. Note the painted FERRYHILL title on the front casing, a throw back to late LNER days when it became a regular practice to paint the shed name on the bufferbeams of engines. The chalked legend on the same casing reads "... Oil ways tested and carbon ??? back ..."

(previous page) Dunfermline WD 'Austerity' No.90489 enters Alloa from the east on 17th July 1966 with a train of empty hoppers from the power station at Kincardine, and which were bound for Alloa yard from where they would go onwards to Polmaise No.3 & 4 Colliery situated on the opposite bank of the Forth. Coal was the lifeblood of this area since the earliest days of the railway and the National Coal Board inherited over two hundred and twenty collieries in Scotland on Vesting day 1st January 1947. By the mid 1960s this number had halved but there was still plenty of traffic for BR to handle. On the left is the former North British Railway built engine shed which was opened in 1885, constructed from local stone. At the time of this photograph the shed had a sub-shed status and its working life was nearly over with closure occurring in the following January. On the right is one of the numerous breweries also found in the Alloa area: Arrol's, Grange, Shore and Younger's to name a few of them.

On the same afternoon of the previous view another Dunfermline allocated engine, this time J38 No.65918, enters the station under the bridge from where the previous photograph was taken. The train again comprises empty coal hoppers but the ultimate destination is uncertain. To the left is the Devon Valley line via Dollar to Kinross. Rationalisation of the railway infrastructure is already taking place, note the disused and lifted bay road on the left. This J38 would shortly be condemned (19th November) and end up at one of the prolific Scottish scrap merchants.

After having just replenished its tender with water WD 90489 again features but this time travelling in the opposite direction en route to Dunfermline shed, light and passing the signal box at the east end of Alloa station. This engine lasted in service until the end of April 1967 and afterwards went to Motherwell Machinery & Scrap at Inshaw. I spent sometime in the signal box during the afternoon lull in the mineral traffic, drinking coffee and learning much about the railway activity in the area. In was in that box where I learned of the derailment of my train which was to take me on to Stirling for a meeting with a lucky A2.

Just across the track from the signal box at Alloa, on the north side of the line, on the 17th July 1966, stood two J38's awaiting the signal to proceed to their next job. Both engines were Dunfermline based and had gone more than three years since their last major overhaul; both would be withdrawn from service by the end of the year.

(opposite) Only weeks after this view of Thornton Junction allocated B1 was got, the engine would be in the scrapyard of Shipbreaking Industries at Faslane. Until then it was employed wherever work could be found as here at the west end of Alloa station, passing through with a mixed train of coaching stock and goods wagons. The B1 had spent all of its working life based in Scotland, going first to Aberdeen Kittybrewster in February 1947 then Ferryhill in May 1949, followed by Dundee in January 1951. Finally it went to Thornton Junction shed in January 1960. It was built in Scotland and had all its repairs and overhauls done in Scottish workshops, mainly Cowlairs. As a result of further rationalisation at this end of the station, one of the bay platforms, formerly used by Caledonian Railway trains, is also redundant.

Bathgate engine shed was situated just to the east of Bathgate (Upper) passenger station and the surrounding area comprised mainly of coal mines and latterly of motor vehicle plants all of which is now but a memory. During my only visit, in July 1964, the motive power depot was still doing good business with numerous ancient 0-6-0's serving the mine runs. However, besides the working engines the place had the air of a 'dump' similar to that at nearby Bo'ness where I had visited the previous year, and the yard was bulging with all types of locomotive from various era's; indeed the place had taken over as the 'transit dump' for Central Scotland now that Bo'ness was closed. J36 No.65309, with its right tender side sheet looking like a patchwork quilt, had only been withdrawn a few weeks before I took this picture. A Bathgate engine since October 1960, the J36 was soon snapped up by the private sector of the scrap metal industry and in September 1964 was sold to the Wishaw yard of Motherwell Machinery & Scrap. By mid-1964 the private scrapyards were certainly gearing up to accepting an even larger influx of mobile scrap and within weeks of locomotives being condemned they were sold and in no time were en route from the shed to the cutters. There was now no need for BR to shunt engines into dumps such as Bo'ness and the days of the out-of-the-way 'dumps' were over.

In an area dominated by coal mining it is inevitable that goods engines will predominate but to find an A3 in the scrap line at Bathgate was something of a shock. Though nameless by now, 60043 formerly BROWN JACK, and the last A3 built, was languishing between a Thompson B1 and an exLMS 2-6-4T. Having worked all of its life from Scottish depots, the A3 had been withdrawn at St Margarets in May 1964 so was a recent arrival here but as I mentioned in the previous caption, the private scrapyards were not 'dragging their heels' anymore and 60043 was already sold, awaiting transit to MM&S's Inshaw yard, not having attained its thirtieth year. On a more personal note, BROWN JACK the racehorse won the Queen Alexandra Stakes 1929 to 1934 and was owned by Sir Harold and Lady Zia Wherner of Luton Hoo, Bedfordshire. My Dad's twin sister was married to the head gardener at Luton Hoo where, in the stables there, were the remains and memorabilia of the great horse. So, I knew all about BROWN JACK from an early age so perhaps that is why I have an intense passion for Gresley's A3 Pacifics.

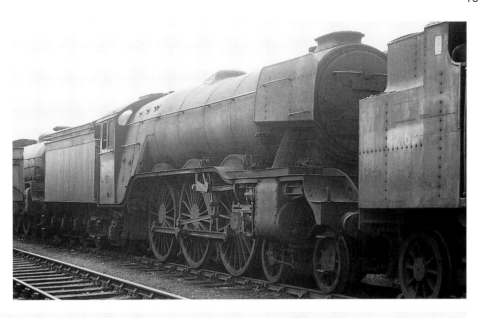

(below) It wasn't all gloom at Bathgate and two J36's noted at work included 65346 (condemned the week after my visit and off to MM&S in September - that curse again) and 65267, here shunting empty 16-ton mineral wagons.

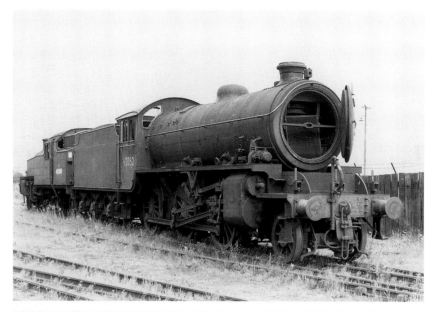

(This page and opposite) A visit to Bo'ness 'dump' on the 17th July 1963 found this sorry collection of withdrawn locomotives awaiting buyers of top grade scrap metal. By the time I got to the place the number of condemned engines had been reduced somewhat, many having already gone to the scrap merchants or BR's own workshops for cutting up. Amongst those locomotives on view were: Stanier Class 3 2-6-2T's 40159, 40177 both ex Dawsholm and withdrawn December 1962, 40200 ex Motherwell and also withdrawn December 1962, all three of these tanks were purchased for scrap by J.H.Connell of Calder in December 1963; K1's 62031, 62052 both ex Fort William and withdrawn December 1962, they would both go into Cowlairs for scrapping in March and April 1964 respectively; J36 65230 latterly of Parkhead and withdrawn October 1962; five ex Parkhead V3's 67611, 67619, 67632, all three withdrawn December 1962, these would all go to Darlington for scrap, 67650 had been withdrawn in August 1961 with collision damage and though due to go to Darlington for scrapping was instead cut up in Scotland, 67676 withdrawn July 1962 and also destined for Darlington. The local kid's used the 'dump' as a playground and were fascinated by my photographic endeavours. No doubt those same youngsters would gape open mouthed when coach parties of railway enthusiasts of all ages and from all over the country kept stopping off to check and record the contents of this mini Barry.

If one locomotive depot in Scotland could boast to having a 'Standard' allocation it must have been Corkerhill in the western suburbs of Glasgow. This one time Glasgow & South Western Railway engine shed opened in 1896 and when I visited the place on 17th July 1966 steam had less than a year to use its facilities before they were banished in the following May. However, many of the BR standard classes were allocated here towards the latter days of steam. Class 3 No.77015 was one of only twenty such engines of which ten were based in Scotland mainly at another ex-G&SWR shed, Hurlford. Looking the worse for standing idle for some time, No.77015 was ex Hurlford but was stored at Corkerhill and had been withdrawn during the month of my visit. In November the engine journeyed one last time to the scrapyard of Messrs Campbell's in Airdrie, just twelve years old.

In the line of stored engines behind 77015 on the 17th July 1966 was Standard Class 4 No.80000 and next to that No.80063. The former had been at Corkerhill since June 1964 having had two previous stints at the depot since appearing new from Derby works in 1952. Ardrossan, Ayr and Hurlford had all had its services over the previous fourteen years. The class leader was not withdrawn until December but it appears here to be out of service. No.80063, on the other hand, was withdrawn just a few weeks after my visit; this Brighton built engine had a more cosmopolitan allocation history going to Saltley shed when new in may 1953 then down to Kentish Town in 1954 followed by Chester shed in October 1956 and onwards to Birkenhead five months later. Its first allocation in Scotland was to Stirling in February 1960, eventually arriving at Corkerhill in July 1964. One wonders if all those fire bricks in the foreground were ever used. Fifteen of the Class 4' tanks were preserved although only one of those came from a Scottish shed; these two took the short journey to Shipbreaking Industries at Faslane.

The Class 4 tender engines with the 2-6-0 wheel arrangement were also part of Corkerhill's allocation. No.76046 was, during my July 1966 visit, one of the more active 'Standards' which although requiring a good clean was nevertheless very identifiable. These particular Class 4's were truly what BR locomotive standardisation was all about, as the class of one hundred and fifteen engines were spread about through all the regions of British Railways working mainly goods traffic but, when occasion arose, they were equally at home on passenger services. This engine had started life at Gateshead shed in March 1955 and after various moves to other North Eastern Region sheds it moved to Scotland in October 1963 based first at Dawsholm, then Grangemouth and finally Corkerhill in October 1965. Withdrawn in May 1967, it was hauled to Campbell's scrapyard in Airdrie in September of the same year. Four of the class were eventually preserved - all being in the right place at the right time.

The smallest of the Standard tender engines were the Class 2's and Corkerhill had just one representative of that class on its books in the shape of 78026 which in July 1966 was looking rather forlorn. A product of Darlington works, it emerged new in June 1954 and was sent to Canklow. In January 1962 the engine came to Scotland, first going to Ayr, then Dumfries and then Stranraer, spending about twelve months at each shed. Corkerhill received the engine in November 1964 and then condemned it in August 1966, a month after my visit. One of the many ironies emerging from the latter days of BR steam locomotion is that Darlington works cut up BR Standard Class 2 No.78015 less than ten years after building it. No.78026's demise was less ironic though nevertheless just as severe as it went to the Old Kirkpatrick yard of Arnott Young in December 1966 for cutting up.

Between them, the Upperby and Kingmoor sheds in Carlisle probably housed every serviceable BR 'Britannia' during those last years of the mid to late 60's. No.70013, minus the OLIVER CROMWELL nameplates was attached to Upperby shed when it visited Corkerhill shed in July 1966. Carrying code 1S44 the engine had probably worked in from the south with a 'Glasgow Fair' returning special which had originated in Blackpool, a popular holiday destination for Glaswegians in those pre-Costa years. 70013 was amongst the largest of the BR Standards and it was also amongst the last handful of working steam locomotives on BR being withdrawn at Carnforth shed in that fateful month of August 1968. Preserved it definately is.

(opposite) On my first visit to Scotland in July 1963 one of the Edinburgh sheds which had much of interest was the former Caledonian establishment at Dalry Road. By now all sorts of motive power could be found stored or working in the strangest of places. Ex-CR McIntosh designed 0-4-4T No.55124 was the last member of its originally ten strong class (CR Nos.19 to 28) and even though it had not worked since its 1961 withdrawal, it was still intact for my visit, except for the lack of a chimney, but shortly afterwards it was hauled away for scrapping. Built in 1895, it is one of the oldest locomotives featured in this album.

(left) **Behind the Caley tank was another withdrawn engine in the shape of ex LNER D49 class No.62712, formerly MORAYSHIRE but minus nameplates in July 63 which was not surprising considering the 4-4-0 had been withdrawn two years previously. Since its withdrawal from Hawick shed the D49 had also done stationary boiler duties at Slateford Laundry. However, the story of 62712 continued when, after a further eighteen months in store it was purchased for preservation in January 1965. The rest is, as they say, history.**

(below) **Further along this line of stored and redundant engines at Dalry Road shed was another former Caledonian engine, this being an 0-6-0, No.57634, one of the ninety-six McIntosh '812' class which were built between 1899 and 1909. All these 3F engines lasted long enough to become BR property but withdrawals started in 1948, with the last engine surviving until 1963.**

(opposite) **In the following year another July visit to Dalry Road took place and the stored engine line had changed from the previous year. No ex-Caley engines and the D49 had gone also but its eventual fate we know about. Two Thompson B1's, 61351 and 61307, now stood forlorn, awaiting better times. The former of the two had been transferred to Dalry Road shed in the second week of the previous month from St Margarets shed (note the 64A shed plate) in the company of 61307 but ten days before my 23rd of the month visit 61351 had been condemned and so would never work again. In September it journeyed south to the BR works at Darlington where it was cut-up; its tender was more fortunate being converted for use as a snowplough. 61307 did not suffer the same fate and was transferred back to St Margarets the day after Dalry shed closed, 3rd October 1965. The B1 worked on for another thirteen months being transferred to Bathgate, Thornton Junction and back to St Margarets in the meantime. However, condemnation caught up on 19th November 1966 and it was sold to Motherwell Machinery & Scrap during December.**

Considering Dalry Road was a former LMS as well as CR shed, the number and variety of ex LNER engines allocated or visiting during the latter years was interesting and none more so than A4 No.60007 SIR NIGEL GRESLEY which had just been transferred from St Margarets to Aberdeen Ferryhill in the few days previous to my visit. Whilst officially allocated to 64A it had latterly been stored at Dalry Road still with its 64A shedplate fiited. On this day it was being steam tested prior to actually going to Ferryhill (some people have all the luck don't they!). Behind the A4's tender is one of the diminutive North British Loco. built 0-4-0 diesel hydraulic shunters which could be seen all over Scotland in the 1960s. The Dalry Road stud consisted of D2754 and D2755. Besides those two there was also half a dozen of the ubiquitous BR 0-6-0 diesel-electric shunters allocated. When the depot closed the two NBL engines went to Leith Central for their remaining few years of life whilst the 0-6-0s went to St Margarets.

My July 1966 trip to Dundee Tay Bridge shed found this J37 on the 70ft articulated turntable which was situated at the eastern end of the shed yard. No.64547 had been a 'recent' allocation to Dundee, arriving at the end of March 1964 from St Margarets where it had spent most of its life except for a seventeen month period at Dalry Road of all places. It was condemned at Dundee on New Years Eve 1966 and went for scrap to J.McWilliam, Shettleston in March of the New Year.

Peppercorn A2 No.60530 SAYAJIRAO had re-allocated to Tay Bridge shed on the last day of July 1964 so I had missed it on that occasion by just a few days. This engine had come to Dundee by way of Polmadie shed and was one of three Peppercorn A2's (the others were 60527 and 60535) which were sent in September 1963 to help out on the West Coast Main Line - Thompson A2/3's Nos.60512, 60522 and 60524 also helped out at the time. By 1966 there was only three of the original fifteen class members still intact, most of the scrapping had taken place during 1962 and 1963. So this was to be their last year of operation. Thankfully, as is well known, one engine was preserved but 60530 was not the lucky race horse, instead, after its November 1966 condemnation it went the way of many elegant Pacifics and other lesser breeds - into the yard of the unforgiving acetylene torch bearers at Motherwell Machinery & Scrap. In its last few months 60530 still appeared to be mechanically sound but although clean, the peeling paintwork had to be seen to be beleived.

(opposite) Just when the tradition of buffing up and even painting the smokebox door hinges, number and shed plates started at Dundee is not known but the shed tried its best to make its engines stand out from the mucky crowd during the latter years of steam on BR. So it was on 22nd July 1964 when I came across Peppercorn A2 No.60528 TUDOR MINSTREL which although covered in a film of road grime still looked presentable. This A2 had come Dundee from Ferryhill in June 1961, its second stint at the shed and it was to return north to Aberdeen in April 1966 for a few weeks before being withdrawn from service. It had in fact spent approximately sixteen of its eighteen year life allocated to Tay Bridge shed.

No.61180 was another B1 which had spent its entire life working in Scotland and Dundee shed had treated it to further identification embellishments on the bufferbeam. This engine had been at Tay Bridge since June 1955 and left for Dunfermline at the end of August 1966 only to return in early November. In late November it moved to Aberdeen but came back to Dundee in March of the following year. It was condemned on the day of the official closure of Tay Bridge shed, 1st May 1967.

Inside Dundee shed on that July 1964 day was the lucky one - 60532 BLUE PETER. Again the relevant buffing and painting helped distinguish the engine as a 62B charge. 60532 was another which had come from Ferryhill in June 1961 and was to return there in December 1966 to be withdrawn later that month.

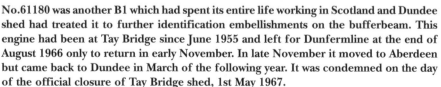

(opposite) A look around the shed in July 1966 revealed other home based engines with their smokeboxes fronts adorned with paint. V2 No.60919 was only six weeks away from being condemned but still the shed staff kept it looking fairly spruce. Likewise 60813, in the background, which had arrived from St Margarets in April. It too had only weeks left before withdrawal.

J37 No.64597 was looking the worse for wear in July 1966. No special treatment on the front of this engine. With its coupling rods missing, along with the smokebox door handles it appears to be non-operational and that was in fact the case as it was never to turn a wheel again in revenue earning service, being condemned on the same day as 64608 and going to the same scrap yard on the same day.

Enginemen at work - with the fireman sitting on the coal and observing the progress of the water filling the tender tank, at the same time keeping his feet above the filler cap so as not to invite a shift with wet feet, his driver with fag in mouth, awaits instructions to turn the stop valve. The B1 was at that time 20th July 1966, based at Thornton Junction shed and had been since April, however, the shed plate of its previous home, 64A St Margarets, is still in evidence. The engine was withdrawn just nine weeks after this pose and one wonders if the shed plate was ever changed.

Standing on the Tay Bridge depot ashpit in July 1964, four locomotives spanning three generations go through servicing. B1 No.61398, two BR Standard Cl.4 tanks, 80124 and 80090 and J37 64597 complete the line. Ex Dunfermline, the J37 was a recent arrival on the Dundee allocation and would soldier on until August 1966. One of the 2-6-4T's, 80124, came new to Dundee in 1955 but would not end its working days there, moving on to St Margarets; 80090 was an immigrant from England (and Wales) being ex Birkenhead in February 1960 and would be withdrawn at Dundee in March 1965. No.61398 was another recent arrival on Dundee's 'books' having been reallocated from Thornton Junction just two days prior to my visit, although the legend 'St Margarets' was painted on the bufferbeam. Note the six-wheel coaches in the background.

In July 1964 Tay Bridge shed also had a line of withdrawn locomotives amongst which were V2's 60825 and 60834. The latter had been at Dundee engine since November 1950 and was withdrawn in the March before my visit. No.60825 had been a recent acquisition from St Margarets arriving on the 27th April and being immediately condemned. It went for scrap at Cowlairs works in September 1964. Note the tender, No.T5298, one of the 4200 gallon Group Standard type with flared copings, one of twenty-eight originally fitted to the D49 class, No.256/62703 in December 1927, in this case, but taken over by V2 No.4812/60841 during November 1938. In May 1957 it went with 60971 until April 1959, then onto 60875 until May 1960, and finally with 60825 from July 1960 to being cut up.

Except for a twenty-four day spell at Perth shed in early 1950, B1 No.61263 had spent all of its nineteen year life allocated at Dundee Tay Bridge shed. In July 1966 it had but five months of work to perform before it was condemned and on this particular day was going through a prolonged period of shed maintenance before being put back into service. The interior views of the sheds were taken from a tripod with the camera set for specific time periods which, had I been on a society or group visit, would have been impossible to achieve due to the hectic schedule of the number-taking brigade who normally whipped around the shed roads in minutes. My more leisurely pace allowed me to get the pictures I wanted and usually meet some of the staff who always had an interest in the photography and the why and wherefore of railway enthusiasm. Tay Bridge shed itself, as mentioned earlier, closed on the 1st May 1967 and stood for a few years before being demolished. It was built by the North British Railway and had opened in 1878. The transverse pitched roof is the original except for more recent corrugated cladding which had replaced the slated cladding. The Caledonian also had a similar establishment just a few hundred yards to the west on the opposite side of the line from Perth - that shed converted to diesel traction in the late 1950s and was in regular use until 1982.

(above) **The Tay Bridge itself got my attention for a couple of frames on 22nd July 1964, and this view of BR Standard 80123 sweeping round the curve at the north end with a passenger working from Tayport, shows the massive solid construction used in this, the second bridge.**

(left) **J38 No.65916, of Thornton shed, rumbles off the bridge and down the gradient towards Dundee with a van train in July 1964. Note the recently refurbished Gresley coach stabled in the carriage sidings - I wonder what happened to that particular one?**

(opposite, bottom) **WD No.90489 we have seen previously working at Alloa a few days before this photograph caught it on the shed yard. It is a Friday afternoon and the yard appears fairly full because most of the work for Dunfermline's engines consisted mine traffic which was carried out mainly during the morning and at night, the afternoon producing something of a lull in activity hence the appearance of so many operational locomotives. Behind is 90041, another resident.**

(above) **Dunfermline had been associated with the WD Austerity 2-8-0s since their introduction in 1943 when they were on loan to the LNER. When the company decided to purchase two hundred of them in 1946 the seal was set and the WD's were there to the end of steam at that shed. Another 2-8-0 which had a somewhat shorter association with Dunfermline was the LNER O6 class (Stanier LMS 8F type) of which from 1946 to the end of 1947 the shed had about a dozen allocated. However, 90039, seen here in the shed yard at Dunfermline on the 21st July 1966, was a latecomer to the stud arriving in October 1963 from Polmadie via a heavy intermediate repair (its last) at Cowlairs works. Six weeks after my visit it was condemned and later sold for scrap to J.McWilliam at Shettleston. Note the miniature snow ploughs lying on the ground, some with engine numbers painted on - J36 No.65327 is visible but that locomotive was by then a pile of scrap having left Dunfermline during May of the previous year for Thornton Junction shed, only to be withdrawn from there in the December.**

On my visit to Dunfermline on the late afternoon of Friday 21st July 1966 I was greeted by the Shed Foreman who after the usual pleasantries were out of the way allowed me to stroll around the shed at my own pace on the proviso that I reported back to him prior to my departure. Of course he was expecting my return within half an hour knowing that taking numbers at a slow pace and having a good look around the place at the same time would only take that long. However, once the tripod is set up and the light meter got to work inside the shed time flies by and just as I was setting up a shot of J36 No.65288, which was tucked away at the back of the shed, the Foreman came into view, full of concern for my well being. When I explained what I had been doing for the last hour he fully understood and relaxed somewhat. Then, to my surprise, he went and got hold of a couple of the on duty staff and instructed them to move the engines blocking the 0-6-0s exit and then drag it outside. This is the resulting photograph which is nicely bathed in the evening sunlight. 65288 was the oldest resident of the shed and had been on the books there since December 1963 and would eventually be one of its last occupants not being condemned until 5th June 1967, over a month after the shed had officially closed. Note the very large tender and engine brake blocks and the lamp on the back - put on, you will note, not for my benefit but in accordance with regulations.

B1's were no strangers to Dunfermline shed and 61407 had been on the books since 12th April 1957 but three weeks after my visit it left the shed for good - not for the scrapyard but to Thornton shed where it was to work until April 1967 and then be sold for scrap. On this day it is undergoing a piston and valve examination and is wearing the compulsory NOT TO BE MOVED sign. Dunfermline shed was quite capable of carrying out these repairs and would often sort out their own engines rather than send them to works. Behind the B1 are a couple of the depots dozen or so diesel shunters whilst out in the yard at the eastern end of the shed was one of the Clayton Type 1 Bo-Bo centre-cab diesels.

New in August 1957, BR Standard Cl.4 No.76109 went to Thornton shed but in January 1960 it moved to Dunfermline shed (Nos.76110 and 76111 later joined it there although the latter went back to Thornton in 1962). This was another engine which was withdrawn just weeks after my visit - perhaps a Jonah like feeling could be described here but it was coming towards the culmination of that period in railway history when the transition from steam to diesel was nearly complete. Note the brickwork in the screen wall of the shed above the door lintels appeared fairly new compared to those bricks in the immediate vicinity of the lintels; the shed had undergone a large refurbishment in the early 1950s and much of the original 1920 building was renewed. at the same time a 70ft turntable was installed and a mechanical coaling plant completed the facilities; a somewhat heavy investment for such a seemingly short period.

(opposite) This J38 was missing its shed plate but the legend on the bufferbeam informs everyone of its home shed. Looking hard worked, the engine is obviously ready for another day (or night) shift at the colliery yards. 65918 was condemned in the November after my visit and later sold for scrap, but it was over forty years old and had probably returned its initial and subsequent costs a number of times - its scrap value figure was not far off its building cost figure in 1926 but in real terms inflation had kicked in during those five decades.

42739 was one of the Hurlford 'Crabs' and carries the large cabside numerals favoured by St Rollox works at repaints. This engine had spend most of its life in England, first at Willesden from new in 1930 then Rugby from 1934 until June 1959 when it re-allocated to the ex-G&SWR shed in the heart of the Ayrshire coalfield. Its arrival 'dead' at Eastfield in July 1966 suggests that it was en route to works (Cowlairs by now as St Rollox was being refurbished for diesel maintenance). Whatever happened at Cowlairs is unknown also a mystery is whether or not the engine went back into service. It was however withdrawn in November so the chances are it was stored, condemned and sold for scrap to G.H.Campbell at Airdrie in May of the following year.

(opposite) Without getting too arty-farty about the picture, I particularly like this study at Dunfermline shed when the sunlight streamed through the roof glass allowing a modicum of work to take place.

One of Polmadie's numerous stud of BR Standard Cl.4 tanks stands at Eastfield minus its pony wheels on 17th July 1966. It was probably on its way to Cowlairs works for repair or decision which as it turned out was against further expenditure and the engine was withdrawn. Its appearance points to the fact that it has been in store for some time and its fate was somewhat inevitable. The engine ended its days at Shipbreaking Industries, Faslane in the following November.

At the Glasgow end of the Aberdeen services, Eastfield shed catered for the needs of the A4's on the three-hour expresses. 60024 KINGFISHER is coaled, watered and appears ready to return north, however, it was in for repairs and examination and although these had just been completed it was another week before it left - when I had gone home!

(*overleaf*) Besides visiting some of the busy railway installations of Scotland in 1963, my parents drove over to Loch Tay and at the western end, where the River Dochart drains into the loch, stood the end of the Killin branch from Killin Junction and thereby stood the engine shed which housed the branch engine for its week long foray away from Perth shed. BR Standard Cl.4 No.80126 was the branch engine on Sunday 14th July and it can be seen poking out into the daylight. The timber built engine shed was erected in 1918 on the site of a previous establishment which had burnt down in October 1917. Just behind me was the timber built station buildings known as Loch Tay which, although having been closed for twenty-odd years, was still in good condition.

(previous page) **With foliage up to, and indeed creeping over and under the track, 80126 pokes out of its shed in July 1963 looking for all intent and purposes like an explorers 'find'. Indeed this out-of-the-way place was a gem but it was obvious that its future was far from assured. It was announced that the branch would be closed on 1st November 1965 but nature intervened, as it does in such places, and a landslide in Glen Ogle on 27th September 1965 hastened the closure by five weeks.**

In order to be always in front of its train, 80126 detached from and left the single carriage on the main line, ran into a spur whereby allowing the guard to release the coach handbrake letting it roll past the siding then stopping to allow the tank engine to couple up and resume normal working. This manoeuvre was carried out at Killin station situated at the bottom of the commencement of the climb to Killin Junction. Known locally as 'gravitating the coach'. The notice on the signal post reads " End of staff section - commencement of yard working." Other Perth based Standard 4 tanks besides 80126 were regularly used on the branch in its latter years including 80092 and 80093; each engine would spend about six weeks on the workings during which it would visit Crianlarich about once a week to collect a wagon of coal for its own use. Prior to Perth shed having responsibility for the Killin branch motive power, Stirling shed would supply one of its Caley 0-4-4T's or even an 0-6-0 tender engine with Caledonian origins.

On Monday 15th July another visit to Killin found the Standard tank waiting to depart from the tiny station to Killin Junction. Some of these branch line stations had a number of useful facilities and Killin could boast a goods yard with a two-ton crane (later upgraded to five-ton). Loch Tay also had goods facilities with a crane of $1\frac{1}{2}$ ton capacity at the end of the short pier jutting into the loch but its passenger services had ceased at the outbreak of war in September 1939.

The BR Standard 9F's were regular visitors to Scotland, mainly from Carlisle, especially during the last four years of steam on BR. Kingmoor's 92249 was seen at Motherwell on 22nd July 1966 replenishing its water prior to its return south.

(opposite) Motherwell shed was one of those stone structures which when built by the Caledonian Railway in 1866 must have looked quite grandiose but the ravages of time and pollution had played havoc with the roof and BR were forced to rebuild the roof and replace the gables with new cladding including corrugated materials which was in plentiful supply in the early 1950s. On 22nd July 1966 the shed was home to numerous Stanier Class 5's with 45359 being one of its latest acquisitions having arrived from Stirling in the month before my visit. Note the painted 66B on the smokebox whilst the Stirling legend still adorns the bufferbeam. Prior to its life at Stirling shed, this engine had started out new in May 1937 at Inverness and stayed there for eleven years before moving south to Stirling. 45359 was withdrawn in May 1967 just a couple of months before the shed closed to steam power. The other Class 5 in view, 44820 had a much more interesting though shorter life starting its career at Derby in December 1944 moving to Holbeck then back to Derby then to Holbeck once again. A move to St Margarets in August 1951 secured its future in Scotland. In May 1954 it moved to Fort William for the summer season traffic then to Perth in December and finally to Motherwell where its ended its days in December 1966. Both engines went to the same Scottish scrapyard during 1967.

The former LMS locomotive depot at Perth stood on the west side of the mainline, south of (General) station, and had been opened in May 1938. The shed itself built to the then standard LMS multiple pitched roof design using lightweight materials such as corrugated sheeting for cladding and to compliment the new depot a mechanical coaling plant, 70ft turntable, and two-road repair shop were also provided. The engine stabling shed consisted eight through roads and here on the yard in July 1966, two of the depot's large allocation of Stanier Class 5's bask in the afternoon sun. Nearest camera is 44797 which was but two months away from withdrawal. This engine, new in September 1947, had spent all of its fairly short life allocated to Perth. No.44998 on the other hand had been built in the same year but much earlier and had gone new to Crewe North in March, then to Rugby in May. It came to Perth in the first month of British Railways and stayed thereafter until withdrawal in April 1967. Lurking in the shed, at the rear of 44998's tender is one of the BRCW Type 2 diesels which became synonymous with the Scottish railway scene after the end of steam. As mentioned previously, the internal combustion machines were not part of my quest at that period.

(*opposite*) Seen two years before and captured on film at Aberdeen, Stanier Class No.44704 stands amongst equals at its home shed in July 1966 with only weeks to go before its services would no longer be required. Still looking as dirty as that day at Ferryhill shed in 1964, at least the front number and shed plates are discernible with the help of paint (perhaps some of the Dundee influence had rubbed off?). Since their introduction in 1934, Perth shed has always had a large allocation of these useful 4-6-0s with sixty or more being on the books at any one time in the 1940's, 50's and early 60's; roughly half the complement of the shed's normal one hundred and twenty strong locomotive fleet.

Further diesel types are lurking in the shadows of this print featuring Class 5 No.44998, and on the left are their fuelling points. When Perth shed closed to steam on the 14th May 1967, the diesels had carte blanche use of the place until October 1969 when they too were evicted. The LMS built shed had replaced the former Caledonian establishment which had stood just a couple of hundred yards north of the new shed and which had been built in 1854. Another LMS engine shed existed at Perth, built by the Highland Railway and situated north of General station. It closed in 1938 and its locomotives and staff transferred to the new LMS shed.

(opposite) A class which arrived fairly late at Perth was the BR Standard Cl.4 tank engines of which No.80028 here was the last one received being allocated in November 1963 from Stranraer. Prior to that this engine had been at Kittybrewster from new in 1952 until June 1961 when it moved south to Ardrossan. Exactly a year later it went to Hurlford, then to Stranraer in June 1963. Withdrawal was in September 1966 - just weeks after my visit. In the background 80092 and 80093 (both saw service on the Killin branch), which had both started life at sheds in England, came to Perth together in February 1960 and they too were condemned in the September after my visit. Funnily the pair went to the same scrapyard together at Airdrie - perhaps they were inseparable. One more engine, 80126, completed the Perth complement and that wasn't on shed in July 1966 but we did see I earlier working the Killin branch.

A last look at one of Perth's Stanier Class 5's - 45475, one of the older members of the fleet, rests in the shed (the motion is well greased and the engine is obviously in store) with 44705 behind it. The carrying of a miniature snow plough in winter was normal practice for Perth engines and evidence of that can be seen by the holes in the bufferbeam and the two brackets beneath - where have those winters gone when it was regarded as normal for trains to meet small (and large) snow drifts during the course of the winter months. Besides the LMS designed Class 5's, Perth had three of the BR Standard Cl.5's (73106, 73107, 73120) during the late 1950's and early 60's - probably one of the largest gathering of 4-6-0s outside of the Western Region.

(above) A general view of Perth shed on the 21st July 1964 with 'Duchess' No.46240 CITY OF COVENTRY taking centre stage amongst a mainly ex LMS gathering. In the background, immediately behind the Pacific stands the two road repair shop with a water tank covering its north end. From new in March 1940, and in streamlined form, 46240 had been based at Camden shed for most of its working life. In September 1963 it was reallocated to Willesden shed where it was put into store for three months before returning to traffic albeit secondary duties. It probably got to Perth via workings to Crewe and later Carlisle.

(right) At the back (south end) of Perth shed on the 14th July 1963 were some interesting engines such as this ex-Caley 4-4-0 No.54482, latterly of Aviemore shed and bound for the scrapyard. Other former Caledonian engines on shed that day included 3P No.54466 and three 2P 0-4-4 tanks, Nos.55204, 55260 and 55269; all had been withdrawn. 2P's 55204 and 55260 had come to Perth in the previous summer to share the Killin branch workings but whether or not they actually got to the branch is unknown, BR Standard Cl.4 tanks having taken over the duties and, by the end of 1962 the pair were condemned anyway. Also at the back of the shed were two Western Region Pannier tanks, Nos.1646 and 1649 which had recently retired from work on the Dornoch branch (withdrawn December 1962) and were en route for scrapping. Unfortunately my camera developed a wind-on fault so depriving me of a pictorial record of the occasion.

CITY OF COVENTRY departs from Perth on the 21st July 1964 with the 2.11 p.m. Aberdeen-Manchester fish train, watched intently by my cousin Michael (in the dark jacket). Sightings of 'Duchesses' working on the WCML was, by this date, becoming something of a rarity and to see a London engine this far north was rare indeed. This particular working would put it on the road for home but only perhaps with a parcels or fast goods train. By the end of the summer timetable 46240 would be withdrawn and at years end would be in the hands of scrap merchants Cashmores at Great Bridge. The fish train had arrived at perth behind A4 No.60023 GOLDEN EAGLE. In the right background a train departs for Dundee West.

Indulging once again with the Gresley A4, we meet 60034 LORD FARINGDON at Perth (General) on Tuesday, 19th July 1966, after its arrival from the north on the 5.15 p.m. three-hour express from Aberdeen to Glasgow. The engine appears to have had something like a cleaning and looks good in the afternoon sun light. During my week long stay the 1.30 p.m. ex Aberdeen was worked by 44703 and 60532, and the 5.15 p.m. ex Aberdeen by 60034. The train has got the green light and the indicator shows the letter M for the main line. Through the arch of the bridge can be seen part of the extensive goods sidings near the engine shed.

Next day, in slightly duller weather conditions, I was waiting for the early evening arrival of the 5.15 p.m. express from Aberdeen when 60034 steams in again at its head. Securing a classic low frontal shot, I proceeded onto the public overbridge to get my next view of the engine *(opposite)*. Luckily, with a crew change and the taking on of water I had time to set up and compose my shot before departure time. Perth was the crew change over point for this train and the driver in charge of the Aberdeen to Perth leg (an ex Caley man, just!) is seen walking away whilst the fireman about to work the Perth to Glasgow leg is at the cab window. The line to and from Dundee, and the alternative route to Aberdeen leads off in the right background.

(above) During my July 1964 trip to Scotland, I managed to secure this shot at Perth (General) of Kingmoor 'Clan' 72008 CLAN MACLEOD proceeding 'light' prior to backing down to the shed after coming off a Carlisle-Perth parcels train on Tuesday the 21st. The last five of the ten 'Clans' finally built were all allocated to Carlisle's Kingmoor shed from new in 1952. The first five, Nos.72000 to 72004 went to Glasgow's Polmadie shed, also from new, and except for a couple of loan periods to the main Edinburgh sheds, stayed there. However, their 'stay' at Polmadie was short indeed - ten years, start to finish. In December 1962 all five were condemned and then, after being stored for many months, were sent over to Darlington works for scrapping. The Carlisle 'Clans' lasted a further three to four year in general and were withdrawn gradually. Now, to say that the Scottish Region of BR wanted to rid itself of steam power sooner rather than later was certainly the case. That perfectly serviceable and capable steam locomotives, only ten years old, should be thrown onto the scrapheap with such obvious hostility and vandalism is unforgivable. That those who 'run' the public purse can be so blatantly wasteful is bloody outrageous. Off with their heads!

Our first 'Jubilee' of the 1966 trip albeit without nameplates. No.45697, formerly ACHILLES, was new in April 1936 and was amongst the last batch of the class to be built. After a one month loan to Crewe North, the 4-6-0 went to Blackpool Central shed in May 1936. Newton Heath then had it a month later until October 1939 when it returned to Blackpool. In September 1952 it moved north to Kingmoor but returned south ten years later to Blackpool. In June 1963 it went to Bank Hall shed and from there to Farnley Junction in February 1964 followed a month later by its final move to Holbeck. It was withdrawn for scrap in September 1967. Besides the **HOLBECK** legend on the bufferbeam the cabside is adorned with the compulsory yellow stripe which effectively banned any locomotive with such markings from working south of Crewe on the WCML.

Kingmoor 9F No.92093 tops up its tender under the Polmadie coaling plant on 17th July 1966 having worked in from the south. Many of these young and very capable engines ended their days at Kingmoor shed some barely ten years old - what a waste. On 2nd November 1963 I photographed this locomotive passing through Nottingham (Victoria) [near my home] on a Woodford-Annesley 'runner'.

(above) **Polmadie could boast to have had over a hundred and twenty 2-6-4 tanks of all types allocated since 1948 and Fairburn No.42277 was typical. On 17th July 1966 the engine is still active, and fairly presentable, although much of its former work was fast disappearing as the Glasgow electric multiple units (Blue Trains) came into use more and more throughout this period moving commuters about in clean, fast new rolling stock.**

(opposite, top) **A general view of Polmadie shed yard in July 1966 with exLMS and BR Standard steam using the southern roads whilst the depot's diesel shunters and other diesel types (Clayton and English Electric Type 1's) hog the north side of the shed. Kingmoor based 'Britannia' No.70035, formerly RUDYARD KIPLING, is another visitor whilst Standard Cl.4 No.76104 is a recent acquisition from Bathgate. The wide, fourteen road shed at Polmadie was a very impressive structure and dated from 1925 when it had replaced a similar sized timber built shed which had been put up in 1875.**

(opposite, bottom) **As mentioned above, Polmadie had a huge fleet of 2-6-4 tank engines at its disposal for most of the commuter services into and out of Glasgow Central to destinations on the south side of the Clyde. Its stud of BR Standard Cl.5 tanks was also quite impressive in size and these two, 80121 and 80058, were part of that stud. In July 1966 both were stored - services no longer required. No.80058 had spent all of its working life from new in January 1955 allocated to the Glasgow depot and had just been condemned prior to my visit. 80121 had been at Polmadie since July 1961 having been stationed at the former Great North of Scotland Railway shed at Keith for most of the time prior to its journey south. It was withdrawn in the June. I'm sure that I once read an article about such matters but a question which always hits me in the face whenever I look at these and similar pictures is - "What happened to all that coal still in the bunkers and tenders of all those thousands of locomotives withdrawn during the 1960s ?"**

(left) Amongst the locomotives stored at Polmadie in the summer of 1966, awaiting sale to scrap merchants, was this Standard Cl.5 No.73055 which went new to Polmadie in June 1954 and after spending all of its working days there, was withdrawn two months before my visit in July. This engine was purchased in the first month of 1967 and was scrapped at the Langloan yard of P.W.McLellan. Buffered up to the Cl.5 is one of the numerous diesel brake tenders which were constructed around a ballasted body utilising old coach bogies and were built to provide extra braking power for diesel locomotives hauling unfitted goods trains. Usually they ran in front of the locomotive and were a common sight during the transition period from steam to diesel and beyond.

(below) We met this Class 5 at Motherwell shed and here it is again some five days prior to that meeting, on the Polmadie turntable, looking as filthy as ever. The fireman, intently controlling the vacuum tractor, is easily able to turn 150 tons of metal just by moving a lever. This turntable was one of two available at Polmadie and was sited at the south-eastern end of the yard.

After my hair raising trip by road from Alloa on the 18th July 1966 (*see* Introduction), I managed to get to Stirling in time to photograph Peppercorn A2 No.60532 **BLUE PETER** as it approached with the 1.30 p.m. from Aberdeen to Glasgow. This job was normally performed by a Ferryhill A4 but only one was working that week. 60532 had just been transferred to 61B and carried that shed plate but the bufferbeam was still adorned with the painted legend 'Dundee'.

A worthy close-up of 60532 as it prepares to depart southwards on the last leg of its journey. Judging from its appearance, Dundee shed had been certainly looking after this engine prior to its recent move to Ferryhill.

In contrast to the previous picture, this is BR Caprotti Standard Class 5 No.73149, a St Rollox engine since new in March 1957, on a Dundee to Glasgow working. The early evening sun at Stirling in July 1966 highlights the grime plastered to this locomotive which, no doubt, would never be cleaned again before withdrawal. In November this engine was transferred to Stirling shed but was condemned in December. Whether or not the engine actually got to Stirling is unknown or, if it did, did Stirling take one look at it a store it until desperate. The Caprotti fitted Standard Cl.5's numbered some thirty engines and these spent most of their short lives at just two sheds (after an earlier equal split between three Regions LM, ScR and WR, and four sheds was eventually deemed unworkable after a few years), Patricroft and St Rollox. The former shed initially had none of the new engines but got the ten Western Region examples in 1958, these being joined in the 1960s by the LMR engines from Holyhead and Leicester. Eventually the Patricroft Caprotti's went on working into 1968 and were amongst the last of BR's operational steam locomotives. Back to the Scottish element though, St Rollox had its batch 73145 to 73154 from new in 1957 and kept hold of them until 1966 when some went to Eastfield, Motherwell and Stirling. The latter shed having 73149, 73150, 73153 and 73154 though only 73154 spent any time there from December 1965 to June 1966 - the other three were transferred (on paper) at the same time and all withdrawn at the same time so probably never made the move. To tie up the story a wee bit more, the three December 1966 withdrawals all ended up at the same scrapyard - Shipbreaking Industries, Faslane.

(*opposite*) **Stirling shed was visited on the 17th July 1963 and it was a nice surprise to find one of Stanier Pacific No.46244 KING GEORGE V on shed, in steam having worked in from Carlisle on the 9.30 p.m. Sutton Coldfield to Stirling Car Sleeper. Put to traffic at Camden shed in July 1940, KGV had been an Upperby engine since June 1958, its main occupation at that time was hauling the heavy West Coast Main Line express passenger trains south to London and north to Glasgow and Perth. By 1963 diesels had all but taken over those duties and the big 8P's were being relegated to work secondary duties such as fish trains, parcels, express goods trains or being put into store for lengthy periods; ten of them had already been cut up at Crewe works and the future for the rest of the class was far from rosy. 46244 itself would go into store in December and be put back to work during the following March but as the summer timetable was about to finish it was withdrawn at Upperby shed on 12th September 1964. Except for a one month loan period in late 1940, KGV had spent all of its fairly short working life at the aforementioned English sheds. It was sold for scrap to the West of Scotland Shipbreaking Co. at Troon.**

(*right*) **A3 60097 HUMORIST was another welcome surprise at Stirling during my July 1963 'bash'. Based then at St Margarets, the thirty-four year old Gresley Pacific was probably on its last working duty because just six days after I captured this photograph of its front end, it entered Doncaster works for a repair which was never undertaken, instead it was condemned on 24th August and cut up. Note the centre valve gear access plate is open which perhaps meant that there was a problem with the valve gear?**

Amongst the last ex Caledonian 4-4-0's still extant in 1963 was 54501 seen with an exCR 'Jumbo' at Stirling in July 1963. Both engines were in a woebegone condition although the 0-6-0 sports electrification warning flashes on its tender.

My first visit to Scotland took in St Margarets depot which was basically split in half by the East Coast Main Line with a large six road shed on the south side of the line and the remains of a small roundhouse on the other side nestling in amongst what was part of the old locomotive works. Thompson B1 No.61350 was the subject of one of my initial exposures on Wednesday 17th July 1963. Seen with the evening sun reflecting off its relatively clean smokebox door, the engine is being prepared to go out on the road. Note the cloud of smoke hanging in the background, a feature of any large engine shed and sometimes the guide in the sky on one's first visit.

A3 No.60101 minus its CICERO nameplates makes a melancholy sight languishing at the side of the shed on that Wednesday evening in July 1963. This Pacific had been condemned three months previously but would not go to the yard that scrapped it until the following summer. 60101 had worked from Scottish sheds since new in June 1930 and had been at Haymarket, Dundee, Eastfield and St Margarets.

(opposite) On my visit in 1963 I did not take a photograph of the engine acting as stationary boiler on the old roundhouse site. However, in July 1964 I made up for that discrepancy and took a photograph of each side of N15 No.69128 which had been withdrawn in October 1962 but, being a St Margarets engine at the time, had taken up SB duties as its boiler (No.26390) was still in good condition even though it had been with the engine since its last Heavy Intermediate repair at Inverurie works in August 1957, when it was still a Ferryhill engine. At the end of 1964, 17th November to be exact, the engine was sold to Motherwell Machinery & Scrap for cutting up. The engine is making plenty of smoke on this glorious summer afternoon, nearly up to its axles in ash and clinker. In the background can be seen one of those Clayton centre-cab Type 1 diesels again.

(left) A3 No.60057 ORMONDE was built in 1925 as an A1 and rebuilt during 1946 and 1947 to A3 standard. Until March 1939 it had been working from sheds in England such as King's Cross, Doncaster and Grantham. Its first Scottish shed was Haymarket and subsequent sheds included Dundee, Eastfield, Carlisle Canal and St Margarets, where I saw it during my July 1963 visit when it was seemingly out of use and extremely grubby. Though not many enthusiasts would agree, the German type smoke deflectors suited these engines though their application rather late in the life of the A3's did nothing to slow the demise of the class. 60057 was withdrawn at the end of October 1963 and went to the same scrapyard as 60101 - Arnott Young at Carmyle.

In amongst the buildings on the north side of the ECML was 'Pug', 68095 which had been withdrawn in the previous December, just eighty years old, and was purchased privately for later preservation. Once very common at St Margarets shed, the tiny 0-4-0ST's used to huddle together around the turntable of the old roundhouse, and some with the wooden bodied tenders which gave them a greater endurance when working away from shed.

(*left*) Though the right hand side of 69128 is in shade, we have a chance to see a bit more of the site on this side of the shed. A couple of dome covers lay on the floor, no doubt left behind by previous 'SB's'; 69128's dome cover is sitting on the side tank awaiting refitting when the time comes for this engine to hand over to another. The number of the SB on the right is unknown but not being attached to a locomotive it has a more permanent shelter acting as a cab. In the left background can be seen the roof of the St Margarets coaling stage on the other side of the ECML - how the shed managed until closure in May 1967 without ever having a mechanical coaling plant seems bizarre.

(*below*) Another blinkered A3, No.60042 SINGAPORE, has its tender full of what appears to be some good quality coal but it had been condemned on Monday 13th July just ten days before my visit. With its connecting rod missing it was going nowhere except for scrap and it did not have to wait too long as during October it was sold to the same yard which took care of 60057 and 60101. This engine was a late arrival in Scotland having spent the majority of it life since new in 1934 working on the old North Eastern Area of the LNER, afterwards the NE Region of BR, being allocated to Aberdeen Ferryhill in April 1963 and then St Margarets in October of the same year. The stay was short indeed. Many years later I became a regular driver of a Hawthorn Leslie saddletank at Rutland Railway Museum - its name is SINGAPORE (one can dream).

When Dalry Road shed closed those locomotives still capable of further service were, in the main, sent to St Margarets and ex-LMS Cl.4 tank No.42691 arrived in October 1965 to complement the other 2-6-4 tanks already in residence at the former North British depot. However 42691 did an earlier stint at St Margarets in 1964 and here on the 23rd July it is making its way out of the rear yard and off shed with the duty foreman not only watching proceedings but helping out with the point levers. It was always dark and smokey behind 64A, even on a bright July afternoon. One wonders what it must have been like to have lived in those tenements in the background - interesting for a railway enthusiast but for anyone else!

The first Peppercorn A1 encountered in these pages is 60152 HOLYROOD which although looking filthy was in fact in the best of health. This A1 came to St Margarets from Haymarket in September 1963 after ten uninterrupted years at the other Edinburgh shed. Previously it had done two short stints at Polmadie whilst being a Haymarket engine from new in July 1949. The massive manual coaling stage was the only ever means of replenishing tenders and bunkers at 64A to the very end of steam in May 1967. Some six weeks after my visit 60152 moved south to York shed where it worked until the end of June 1965 when it was condemned. This locomotive is unique in this album by being the only one specifically illustrated that was not broken up in a private Scottish scrapyard instead its met its fate in a private Black Country scrapyard (61351 at Dalry Road was broken up at a BR works so does not count).

(*below*) Outside the shed on Friday 22nd July 1966 Stanier Class 5 No.45483 stands on the ash pits after a visit to the coal stage and is being got ready for another main line turn. This 4-6-0 came to St Margarets in October of the previous year when Dalry Road closed - St Margarets was by now becoming a very cosmopolitan depot if it wasn't already. Having spent all of its life working in Scotland since going to Polmadie when new in October 1943, it certainly finished its life on a wrong note doing stationery boiler duties at Craigentinny carriage sidings during November and December, the month in which it was condemned. On the opposite side of the main line, on the old roundhouse shed site, can be seen the tender of 65234.

(*above*) My July 1966 visit to St Margarets took place on the morning of Friday 22nd, and one of the first places I visited was the old roundhouse site on the north side of the main line, to see what engine was being used as the 'mobile' stationary boiler. What a nice surprise - J36 No.65234 which had moved to Edinburgh in September 1964 from Bathgate to take over this duty from N15 No.69128. The J36 carried on this work until 22nd April 1967 when it was inevitably condemned, then sold for scrap at the end of July. This engine is the oldest one illustrated here - built 1891, a real veteran. Note the piece of timber holding up the steam pipe is now vertical. Also note the roof on the old workshop building in the background appears to be fire damaged - the end was fast approaching. In not too many years from when this scene was captured a new purpose built athletics stadium would be built on this very site, in time for the Commonwealth Games.

This view of St Margarets yard on 22nd July 1966 might lead one to believe this was an ex LMS depot with two Fairburn 2-6-4T's and a Black 5 hogging the pits in front of the shed but some of the original residents are inside the shed. 42273 was another Dalry Road orphan which only St Margarets would take in. After the 1966 Summer Timetable had finished this less than twenty years old engine would be condemned.

(opposite) Finishing off my last visit to St Margarets I got the tripod set up inside the shed to capture on film this very clean Gresley V2 which was rubbing shoulders with some of the depots numerous diesel shunters. No.60955 had come to 64A in May 1964 from Ferryhill shed after a sixteen year spell in Aberdeen prior to which it had served through the war years and immediately afterwards at Haymarket depot. On the 26th September after my visit this V2 was condemned and shortly after purchased for scrap. One is left wondering which engine shed in Scotland started the ritual of painting smokebox number plates, shed plates, hinges, handles and door stops?

(previous page) **The day before my final visit to St Margarets I went to Thornton Junction shed and was pleasantly surprised to see some of the older North British engines still around. J36 No.65327 was inside the shed appearing to be receiving some type of repair concerning coupling rods, brakes and buffers and on which all work had ceased some time previously but in fact it had been 'cannibalised' for spares. This J36 had come to Thornton in May 1965 from Dunfermline and still carries its 62C shed plate. It was condemned in November 1965 and was being prepared for its final journey to Motherwell Machinery & Scrap at Wishaw, the company who had purchased it during the same month as my visit. The six road Thornton Junction depot, 62A, or just plain Thornton was opened in 1933 as a replacement for an earlier four road building built in 1896. The LNER invested heavily in the facilities here with a mechanical coaling plant, 70ft diameter turntable and a repair shop which undertook some fairly substantial work, such as casual light repairs, thereby lessening works visits for some of its engines. The shed building was steel framed as can be seen in this view; cladding was corrugated sheet steel. Note the nice wide spacing between the roads giving the shed's fitters and photographers plenty of room and light to work in.**

J37 No.64606 had been a Thornton engine since November 1964. On the day of my 1966 visit it was languishing on the storage lines having been withdrawn the previous week. It was sold for scrap in September and would by then have got a set of wheels from somewhere to enable it to undertake its last journey. The graffiti on the middle splasher reads … "DR Boxes Packed"… The driving wheel axle boxes will have had steel or wood packing pieces inserted between them and the frames to keep the engine level after removing the front wheel set as all the weight is now unsupported at the smokebox end. That legend on the cab side reads …"Keep in mid gear" - to avoid disturbing the crank axle.

J36 No.65345 was, in July 1966, allocated to Bathgate shed and would be reallocated to Thornton Junction in December 1966. However, although in the books it said Bathgate shed, it was Thornton Junction which was using the sixty-six year old veteran on stationary boiler duties. The tender is one of the rare extended cab types which shows evidence of patching on its side sheets. Note that the coal is stacked fairly high which was probably undertaken by the depot's ash pit grab crane, although highly unlikely, man power could have been used. BR was often accused of wasting taxpayer's money but one glance at the scrap bins reveals a useful second life for worn out timber sleepers. I particularly like this view which not only conveys a hot midday of a British summer but also man's use of equipment and materials for jobs which they were not initially designed to do. The J36 was condemned in June 1967, some time after the shed officially closed so it must have carried on with these duties whilst the place was being cleared out. There is one word prominent twice on the picture which tells the fate of 65345 in Carmyle later in the year.

(above) Two of the shed's recent acquisitions in 1966 were these two B1's, both arriving on 24th April (along with 61344, 61347, 61349), 61099 from Bathgate and 61354 from St Margarets. The latter engine was one of those loaned to the Southern Region for a week May 1953 when there was a problem with the Pacific's. 1946 vintage No.61099 was to be condemned in September and sold the following month for scrap to the Faslane firm of Shipbreaking Industries. No.61354, the younger of the two, faired slightly better and was reallocated to Dundee shed in November and worked from there until the end of April 1967 when it too was condemned.

(right) Another J37 which had been condemned prior to my visit was 64588. This engine had ATC fitted at its last general repair in May 1963. The fence at the cab end of the tender was a fairly recent addition and was provided to prevent the crew climbing onto the tenders in electrification areas such as Glasgow. Weather protection for the crew was provided by the storm sheet seen rolled up against the plate attached to the rear of the roof. Note the worn out ash grabs littering the ground.

At a large and rambling depot like Thornton Junction it took some time to get around the place, especially if the camera, tripod and light meter are being employed regularly along with pencil and notebook so, it was a good idea to take time and digest all the surrounding scenes. In 1966 it was even more important to savour the steam depot because we all knew that it was rapidly disappearing from our lives. Each week would bring the news of another handful of closures and a bucketful of locomotive withdrawals. This view captures not just B1 No.61344, a Thornton engine for at least three months but still wearing its 64A shed plate, but the tender of the WD on the right, the water cranes, and the line of stored and withdrawn locomotives on the far side of the yard.

(next page) Note the concrete and glass winding tower in the background of this picture. This belonged to next door neighbour Rothes Colliery which in 1966 had been closed for about ten years and which never actually fully opened. Sinking of the shafts for the new colliery started in 1947 and it was planned that production in 1954 would bring 1,000 tons of saleable coal a day to the surface and by 1965 this figure would be upwards of 6,000 tons a day. 3,000 men were to be employed and the cost in excess of two million pounds (1947 prices). However, during development of the coal faces a flood occurred for which the flow was impossible to stem. After numerous attempts and years of pumping the faces remained under water and so the decision to close the colliery was taken. The towers remained for many years even after Thornton Junction shed itself was demolished in the 1970s.

Occasionally Thornton Junction's steam breakdown crane was called upon to perform a duty other than picking up locomotives and rolling stock as the result of an accident. Such was the case on the afternoon of 21st July 1966 when one of the carriages of an Edinburgh to Glasgow Inter-City diesel multiple unit required lifting to replace a bogie. J38 No.65921 attends to the needs of the crane.

A general view of the servicing yard with the wet ash pits nearest and the coaling plant dominating the right background. Two of Thornton's WD 2-8-0's and a J38 make use of the facilities. With the investment made in this place by the LNER it is obvious that they envisaged expansion of the depot as the nearby coalfield expanded. In 1956, to handle the extra coal expected by the increased production at two local collieries Seafield and Westfield (opencast) and the yet to come on stream new colliery at Rothes, the Scottish region opened a new yard ready to handle up to 3,000 wagons a day. Thirty-five sorting sidings were laid with storage space for 2,300 wagons. The seventy-eight acre Thornton yard, as it was known, also had three Reception roads for both Up and Down directions. Throughput during the first year of opening amounted to the equivalent of 1,800 wagons a day and by 1958 just over 10,000 wagons a week used the yard. However, the magic figure of 3,000 wagons a day was never attained, perhaps the disastrous flooding of Rothes colliery and the loss of its output did make all the difference.

(*opposite*) To capture the scene inside an engine shed meant that you could basically capture the atmosphere and perhaps the ambience of the place. This view of B1 No.61347 at Thornton conveys much of the atmosphere and the presence of WD No.90117 in the background makes a more pleasing picture. The nearest two roads with pits tended to be used for major repairs, note the connecting rod on the floor by the driving wheels. Those of us who were lucky enough to experience a visit to one of BR motive power depots during the days of steam will certainly remember the unique and never to be felt again emotion found inside a working shed.

Besides visiting the Edinburgh sheds on my first Scottish jaunt in July 1963, I spent some time watching the rail traffic pass through gardens at Princes Street and finding vantage points to observe the traffic entering and leaving Waverley station at either end. At the eastern end of the station, after climbing the steps, known as "Jacob's Ladder" from Calton Road running below the railway, I captured this overhead view of A4 No.60016 SILVER KING entering the station with a train from the south. The A4 was shedded at Gateshead at the time of this photograph but by the end of the year it would go first to St Margarets for a couple of weeks and then, on a more permanent basis, to Aberdeen Ferryhill to work the Glasgow expresses until it was withdrawn in March 1965. Note the amount of coal still available in the non-corridor tender.

BR Standard Cl.4 No.76104, of Aberdeen Ferryhill shed, and B1 No.61244 of St Margarets shed, enter the tunnel beneath the Scottish National Gallery and The Mound with a train for Aberdeen on Thursday 18th July 1963. It was still possible at this time to see lots of steam hauled trains using Waverley although diesel multiple units had taken over many of the 'local' services, the medium and long distance trains had plenty of variety. It is hard to believe now, but the 2-6-0 at the head of the train was only six years old when I saw it that day.

After its short trip to Haymarket shed where it had its tender topped up with coal and water, Gateshead A4 No.60016 is back at the station to work an evening express to the south. Here the fireman looks out for the signal to enable the Pacific to back onto its train.